THE BUILDING OF THE
GOLDEN GATE
BRIDGE

BY ARNOLD RINGSTAD

Published by The Child's World®
1980 Lookout Drive • Mankato, MN 56003-1705
800-599-READ • www.childsworld.com

Photographs ©: AP Images, cover, 1, 20, 22, 26; Library of Congress, 6; Shutterstock
Images, 9, 18; Everett Historical/Shutterstock Images, 10; From the holdings of the
Golden Gate Bridge, Highway and Transportation District, 12; Carsten Reisinger/
Shutterstock Images, 14; Bill Florence/Shutterstock Images, 16; Underwood Archives/
UIG Universal Images Group/Newscom, 24; Dean Birinyi/iStockphoto, 25;
iStockphoto, 28

ISBN 9781503816404
LCCN 2016945637

Printed in the United States of America
PA02321

ABOUT THE AUTHOR

Arnold Ringstad is the author of more than 50 books for kids. He likes to read
about amazing feats of engineering. He lives in Minnesota.

TABLE OF CONTENTS

FAST FACTS

- Location: San Francisco, California
- Construction began: January 5, 1933
- Construction ended: April 27, 1937
- Cost: $27 million
- Length of central span: 4,200 feet (1,280 m)
- Height of towers: 746 feet (227 m)
- Purpose: to carry vehicles and pedestrians across the Golden Gate, the **strait** of water that divides San Francisco from the Marin Headlands
- Materials: concrete and steel
- Special features: was the longest suspension span in the world until the completion of the Verrazano–Narrows Bridge in New York City in 1964
- Engineers: Joseph Strauss, Charles Ellis, Leon Moisseiff, and Irving Morrow

TIMELINE

1921: Michael O'Shaughnessy and Joseph Strauss present a plan to build a bridge across the Golden Gate.

1930: Local voters agree to spend money on the bridge.

January 1933: Construction of the anchorages and piers begins.

January 1935: Both piers are completed.

June 1935: Both towers are completed.

May 1936: Workers complete construction of the bridge's two main cables.

July 1936: Crews begin building the roadway outward from the towers.

November 18, 1936: The roadway construction meets in the center of the bridge.

May 27, 1937: The official opening ceremony for the Golden Gate Bridge is held.

Chapter 1

THE GOLDEN GATE

Michael O'Shaughnessy stood in line for a **ferry**. He was growing impatient. The year was 1916, and O'Shaughnessy was an engineer for the city of San Francisco, California. The growing city was noisy and busy. On weekends, O'Shaughnessy liked to get away to the quiet hills and forests of Marin County. Just a mile (1.6 km) of water separates Marin County from San Francisco. This strait is known as the Golden Gate.

Ferries carried people back and forth. But by 1916, the ferries were overloaded. Too many people wanted to use them, and they were often delayed. O'Shaughnessy wondered if there was a better way to cross the Golden Gate.

One way might be to build a bridge. Luckily, O'Shaughnessy knew a bridge engineer. His name was Joseph Strauss, and he had built many bridges around the country. The two men started developing a plan. They discovered that the challenges ahead were huge. The strait is 300 feet (91 m) deep. High waves from the Pacific Ocean create rough conditions in the water. At the same time, cold winds whip through the strait. Fog **corrodes** metal and blocks people's vision. The area is also rattled by earthquakes. The engineers had their work cut out for them.

They were finally ready to present their plan in 1921. But many groups were against it. Naval officers argued that an enemy might bomb the bridge and knock it down. If that happened, the fallen bridge would block the entrance to the bay. Others worried the bridge would ruin the natural beauty of the Golden Gate. And the ferry companies believed the bridge would harm their businesses.

Strauss felt he could overcome the engineering challenges. He knew the biggest obstacle would be to convince the people of San Francisco that the bridge was needed. He said, "If the people of San Francisco and other communities are willing to spend the money, the Golden Gate could be bridged by 1927."[1]

Debates and delays went on for years. People argued over how to pay for the bridge, how to design it, and how to build it. Even O'Shaughnessy eventually turned against the plan. But Strauss stuck by it. The two engineers became political enemies. However, the decision to build the bridge was not up to them. Local voters had their say in 1930. They approved the bridge. Strauss was named the project's chief engineer. Now, it was up to him to actually build it.

Strauss wanted sole credit for the bridge. But he brought on many other experts to help him. Some were fellow bridge engineers. They checked the math to make sure the structure would be sturdy. Others were **geology** professors. They went to the site and drilled into the rock. They tested its strength to make sure it could hold the huge bridge's weight. Finally, some were architects. They helped give the bridge its famous design. Together, Strauss and his team put together a detailed plan.

By 1933, they were ready to begin construction. One of the bankers who provided money for the project asked Strauss how long the bridge would last. Strauss replied, "Forever."[2]

▲ A statue of Strauss now stands near the Golden Gate Bridge.

Chapter 2

SOLID FOUNDATIONS

In January 1933, workers began digging in the ground on both sides of the Golden Gate. They used heavy machinery to clear away soil and rock. Crews dug down all the way to solid **bedrock**. Then they began filling the spaces with concrete and steel. These structures were the bridge's anchorages. The anchorages were critical parts of the bridge. They would hold the bridge's cables to the ground. And the cables would hold up the bridge itself.

◀ **Construction of the south pier was very complicated.**

Two huge towers would hold the bridge's cables high in the air. The north tower would be on the Marin side. The south tower would be on the San Francisco side. Each tower would be built offshore rather than on land. This created major challenges. Before the towers themselves could be put up, workers had to build large concrete piers to support them.

Building the north pier was fairly simple. It was located close to the Marin shore in shallow water. Workers built walls around the construction area. Then they pumped the water out. This gave them a dry place to work. They poured in tons of concrete using pipes that looked like huge elephant trunks.

The south pier was a much bigger challenge. It was located more than 1,000 feet (305 m) offshore in deep water. Divers jumped off **barges** into the cold, dark water. They wore heavy suits with metal helmets. Oxygen for breathing was pumped down to them through hoses. The divers searched for smooth spots on the floor of the strait where the pier could be attached. Once they found good spots, the divers returned to the surface. Workers used 120-foot (37-m) tubes to drop explosives down to the spots. They then dropped in heavy weights after the explosives, shoving them deep into the underwater rock.

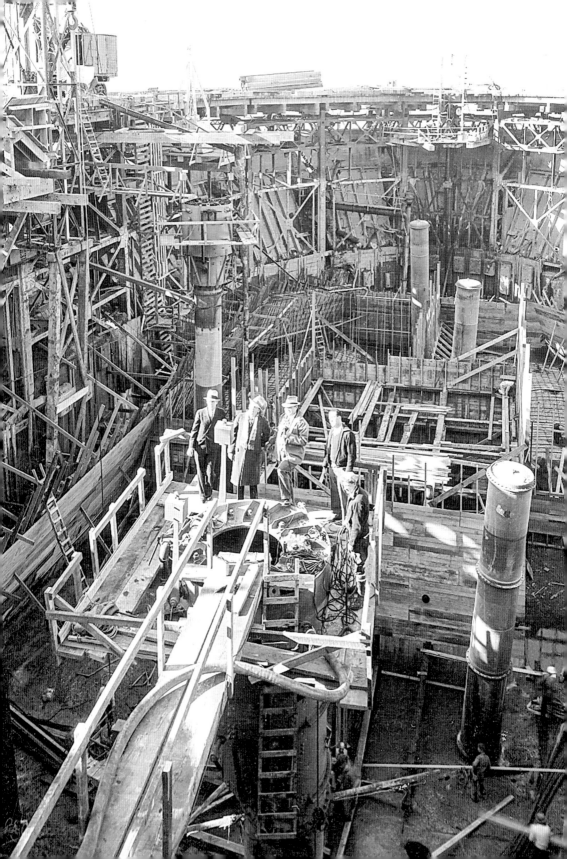

The explosives blew up, clearing off the floor of the strait so that the pier could be safely attached.

The explosions created strong waves. This made the barges rock back and forth. One worker said, "the deck of that barge would lift sometimes six feet, and you'd see some guy turn green."[3] Fish, stunned by the enormous blast, floated to the surface. The seasick workers watched as seagulls flew in to feast on the stunned fish.

The next step in building the south pier was the fender. This was a huge concrete oval the size of a football field. The structure, sometimes called the giant bathtub, was put into place at the building site. It was lowered down to rest on the ocean floor. Then the water was pumped out. With the harsh waters of the strait blocked off, workers could put together the pier. It slowly rose up from the sea. By January 1935, both piers were finished.

◄ **After the water was pumped out, people could work below sea level without getting wet.**

Chapter 3

CONSTRUCTING THE TOWERS

Now it was time to build the bridge's towers. They were constructed from large steel boxes called cells. Barges carried cells out to the piers. Workers at the piers operated powerful cranes and **derricks**. They lifted the cells off the barges and moved them into place on the pier.

At the noisy worksite, it was impossible for the men to talk to one another. To guide the pieces into the right spots, they used loud bells and hand signals. Once a piece was in place, inspectors walked around it to check how well it fit. If there were any gaps, a team of workers would grind away at the cell's edge until everything fit perfectly.

The workers connected the cells together with bolts as they stacked them. But to make the tower strong, they used **rivets**. Riveters worked in teams. Some of the men were outside the tower, and some crawled inside the tower. The towers were dark and mazelike inside, and it was easy to get lost. The banging and crashing noises of construction echoed through the cells, damaging workers' hearing. Workers inside the towers breathed in poisonous fumes created by the paint.

Outside, a worker heated up a small steel cylinder that had a widened end. Then he tossed the white-hot rivet into a pipe that carried it into the tower. Inside, a worker caught the chunk of steel with a funnel and pulled it out with tongs. He placed the rivet into a hole in the wall. Then he held an iron bar firm against the widened inside end. When the worker outside saw the end of the rivet appear, he used a tool to pound the rivet, flattening the head and holding it in place.

With both ends widened, the rivet held the steel cells together permanently. Riveting teams repeated this process over and over for months.

Strauss admitted it could be hard to climb through the dark mazes in the towers. He said, "Although I designed this weird labyrinth, I doubt if I could find my way out of it, even with the aid of the 26-page manual issued to direct the watchmen who inspect the towers."[4]

The riveters themselves soon got used to finding their way in the towers. One worker remembered, "The riveting gang got so they could go through there just like mice."[5]

As the towers grew, workers moved the cranes and derricks higher and higher. By June 1935, both towers were finally finished.

◀ **Each tower is held together by approximately 600,000 rivets.**

Chapter 4

SPINNING THE CABLES

Looking out over the bay, San Francisco residents could now see the bridge's two enormous towers standing in the Golden Gate where there was once only open water. But there was still much work to be done. Strauss designed the structure as a suspension bridge. This meant strong cables would support the bridge's weight. The design called for two main cables.

Each one would begin at an anchorage, go up to the top of one tower, droop down in a U shape, go up to the top of the other tower, and end in the anchorage on the opposite side. The next job for the workers was to add these cables.

Just like everything else about the bridge, the cables were huge. John Roebling and Sons, the top cable-making company in the world, designed them. Roebling's engineers drew up plans for some of the strongest cables ever built. They were made of steel wires about as thick as a pencil. Workers bunched groups of wires into strands. These strands were then bunched into a massive cable more than 3 feet (92 cm) thick.

Strauss and the engineers at Roebling knew these cables would be far too heavy to lift into place. Instead, they had to be strung one wire at a time across the span. For months, workers gradually built these strands into the completed cables. High above the bay, the men worked on a wooden catwalk between the towers. The people working on this walkway risked falling hundreds of feet into the choppy waters below. In the windy, slippery conditions, they had to take extra care to keep their balance.

▲ The bridge's main cables were completed by the end of
May 1936.

Strauss sent out a proud announcement when work on the

cables began. "On Monday, November 11, the first wire of the

west cable was pulled across from the Marin side," he said.[6]

The task ahead was huge. There were many thousands of cables left to go. The process of running the wires back and forth across the span was known as spinning the cables. Three-wheeled devices rolled along existing wires from the anchorages up to the towers. They carried one new wire at a time. The devices met in the middle of the bridge. There, workers quickly swapped the wires so they could complete their long journeys to the opposite side.

Once the strands were completed, a powerful **hydraulic** machine compressed them together. Workers wrapped iron bands around the cable to hold the strands in place.

Originally, the bridge designers planned to spend 14 months on cable-spinning. But the engineers and workers found ways to speed up the work. They eventually had six of the spinning machines going at a time. Workers became skilled at moving the wires around to the correct spinners. As a result, they finished the job an amazing eight months early.

There was one more step to complete before the roadway could be added. Workers attached 250 thick steel ropes to the cables. The ropes dropped down to an even length. They would be used to support the roadway.

Chapter 5

BUILDING THE ROADWAY

By July 1936, it had been more than three years since the first concrete was poured at the anchorages. Since then, workers had built huge piers in the strait. They had put up giant steel towers. And they had spun thousands of miles of wires. The next step, the roadway, would finally complete the bridge.

One day, fog blanketed the strait and left the steel structure wet and slippery. As worker Al Zampa walked across the steel, he took a step and slipped. Zampa's coworkers watched in horror as he tumbled down toward the water. A fall from this height is often fatal.

But Zampa landed in a large safety net that hung beneath the bridge. Though injured, Zampa survived. The net was one of several safety measures the bridge engineers had put into place. Strauss was highly concerned with safety. He ordered his workers to wear hard hats and tie themselves in place with safety lines. He also made sure they didn't try to show off on the high, dangerous steel structure. Strauss said, "To the annoyance of the daredevils, we fired any man who stunted on the job."[7] A total of 19 men were saved by the net. One worker said, "There's no doubt the work went faster because of the net. It gave men a little security."[8]

Still, there were some deaths during construction. The first came on October 21, 1936. A falling crane crushed a worker. The second and final fatal accident happened on February 17, 1937. A work platform with several men on it collapsed. The platform was caught by the net, but only for a moment.

▲ **Workers built the roadway outward from the towers in both directions.**

The weight was too much for the net to hold, and it ripped through. Worker John Marders remembered the terrifying sound it made. "When the scaffold hit the net it sounded like a clap of thunder, followed by the rat-tat-tat of a machine gun, only louder," he said.[9] Ten men died in the fall. A memorial near the bridge is dedicated to the workers who died to build the great structure.

More than 2 billion vehicles have crossed the Golden Gate ▶ Bridge since it opened.

Chapter 6

OPENING DAY

The two roadway crews working toward the center met on November 18, 1936. Riveting teams carefully lined up the last two steel pieces. They slammed the red-hot rivets into place. Now the steel frame of the bridge spanned the entire Golden Gate. Next, workers added concrete over the steel frame. Finally, they paved the road with asphalt. They finished by April 1937. At last, the bridge was ready for its grand opening.

As visitors approach the bridge today, one of the first things they notice is its striking color. The reddish-orange color is now famous, but it was not always part of the plan. Different groups wanted different colors. Some engineers wanted a simple gray color. The U.S. Navy wanted the bridge to have yellow and black stripes. This pattern would make the bridge easily visible from ships. The Army Air Forces wanted red and white stripes so the bridge could be seen from the air. Strauss and his team eventually picked a shade called International Orange. It makes the bridge stand out against the blue waters and sky.

The official opening day for the Golden Gate Bridge was May 27, 1937. It was called pedestrian's day. Only people, and no vehicles, would be allowed to go on the bridge. When the bridge opened that morning, people rushed to be among the first to cross it. Approximately 200,000 people showed up. At 10:00 in the morning, Strauss himself arrived. He emerged from a black car, and the crowd cheered. Strauss liked to write poetry, and he shared a poem he had written for the opening. The first line read, "At last, the mighty task is done."[10] Later that day, U.S. Navy airplanes soared over the bridge. U.S. Navy ships sailed under it, into the bay. The celebrations continued in the city for several days.

GOLDEN GATE BRIDGE AT A GLANCE

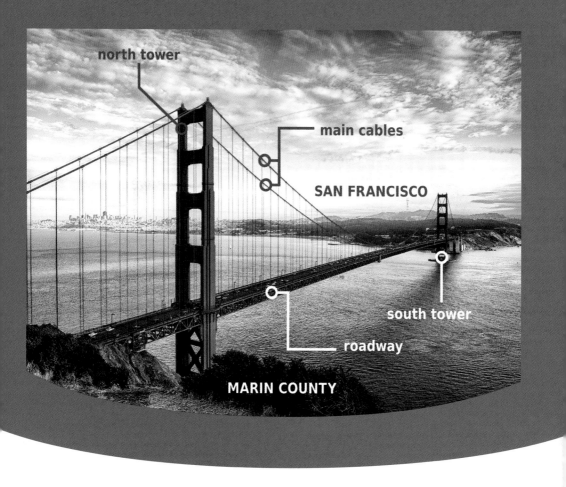

north tower

main cables

SAN FRANCISCO

south tower

roadway

MARIN COUNTY

Joseph Strauss died the next year, in May 1938. Three years later, a life-size bronze statue of Strauss was installed near the bridge in his memory. His bridge has become an important symbol of San Francisco and the United States.

The Golden Gate Bridge opened the way for the growth of cities on the Marin side of the bay. It made travel back and forth across the bay much faster and easier. Since the Golden Gate Bridge opened, more than 2 billion vehicles have traveled across it.

THINK ABOUT IT

- Some people argued that a bridge across the Golden Gate would destroy the strait's natural beauty. After looking at photos of the bridge and of the strait before construction, what do you think?
- The Golden Gate Bridge's color is famous. But during the planning process, different colors were suggested for the bridge. Can you imagine what it might look like in these colors? Would it be as popular as it is today if it were colored gray, or if it had yellow and black stripes?
- The Golden Gate Bridge was built in the 1930s, long before the invention of robots, cell phones, drones, and many other high-tech devices. How might such modern tools be used if the bridge were built today?

GLOSSARY

barges (BARJ-iz): Barges are wide, flat ships designed to carry large or heavy loads. Pieces of the Golden Gate Bridge were brought to the site by barges.

bedrock (BED-rock): Bedrock is the layer of solid rock underground that is often covered by soil or other looser materials. The bridge's anchorages were built atop bedrock.

corrodes (kuh-ROHDZ): Something corrodes when chemical processes gradually break it down and destroy it. Salt water corrodes steel.

derricks (DAYR-iks): Derricks are structures used to lift other objects. Workers used derricks to lift parts of the bridge into place.

ferry (FAYR-ee): A ferry is a boat that carries people from place to place, often over short distances. Before the Golden Gate Bridge was built, people used a ferry to cross the strait.

geology (jee-OL-uh-jee): Geology is the study of Earth's surface and the rocks and structures beneath it. Geology experts studied the ground near the Golden Gate to make sure it could support the heavy bridge.

hydraulic (hy-DRAW-lik): Hydraulic means powered by water pressure. Workers used hydraulic machines to compress many wires into single cables.

rivets (RIV-its): Rivets are metal cylinders that are heated and pounded into place to hold two metal parts of a structure together. There are more than a million rivets in the towers of the Golden Gate Bridge.

strait (STRAYT): A strait is a narrow water passage between two large bodies of water. The Golden Gate is a strait between the Pacific Ocean and San Francisco Bay.

SOURCE NOTES

1. "Complete Program Transcript." *American Experience: Golden Gate Bridge.* PBS, 2013. Web. 19 Apr. 2016.

2. John Van der Zee. *The Gate: The True Story of the Design and Construction of the Golden Gate Bridge.* New York: Simon and Schuster, 1986. Print. 160.

3. John Van der Zee. *The Gate: The True Story of the Design and Construction of the Golden Gate Bridge.* New York: Simon and Schuster, 1986. Print. 183.

4. Richard Dillon. *High Steel: Building the Bridges across San Francisco Bay.* Millbrae, CA: Celestial Arts, 1979. Print. 84.

5. John Van der Zee. *The Gate: The True Story of the Design and Construction of the Golden Gate Bridge.* New York: Simon and Schuster, 1986. Print. 195.

6. John Van der Zee. *The Gate: The True Story of the Design and Construction of the Golden Gate Bridge.* New York: Simon and Schuster, 1986. Print. 242.

7. Richard Dillon. *High Steel: Building the Bridges across San Francisco Bay.* Millbrae, CA: Celestial Arts, 1979. Print. 88.

8. John Van der Zee. *The Gate: The True Story of the Design and Construction of the Golden Gate Bridge.* New York: Simon and Schuster, 1986. Print. 263.

9. Richard Dillon. *High Steel: Building the Bridges across San Francisco Bay.* Millbrae, CA: Celestial Arts, 1979. Print. 93.

10. "Strauss Poems." *Golden Gate Bridge.* Golden Gate Bridge Highway & Transportation District, 2015. Web. 5 Apr. 2016.

TO LEARN MORE

Books

Eggers, Dave. *This Bridge Will Not Be Gray*. San Francisco, CA: McSweeney's, 2015.

Latham, Donna. *Bridges and Tunnels: Investigate Feats of Engineering*. White River Junction, VT: Nomad Press, 2012.

Wearing, Judy. *Golden Gate Bridge*. New York: Weigl, 2010.

Web Sites

Visit our Web site for links about the Golden Gate Bridge: childsworld.com/links

Note to Parents, Teachers, and Librarians: We routinely verify our Web links to make sure they are safe and active sites. So encourage your readers to check them out!

INDEX